GEORGE BENJAM

ANTARA

for 2 flutes, 2 computerised keyboards and ensemble

(1985-7)

FABER 𝆑𝆑 MUSIC

© 1993 by Faber Music Ltd
First published in 1993 by Faber Music Ltd
3 Queen Square London WC1N 3AU
Music processed by Richard Emsley using the
Sibelius 7 system designed by B & J Finn
Cover design by M & S Tucker
Cover photograph Centre Georges Pompidou
© Marjorie Morrison/Architectural Association
Printed in England by Caligraving Ltd

Antara was commissioned by IRCAM for the tenth anniversary of the Pompidou Centre. The first performance was given by the Ensemble Intercontemporain conducted by the composer, in the Espace de Projection, IRCAM on 25 April 1987.

Antara is recorded by the London Sinfonietta conducted by the composer on Nimbus Records NI 5167 (CD & Cassette).

The composition and premiere of Antara was the focus of a BBC film 'Towards Antara' for Omnibus directed by Barrie Gavin, which was first shown on BBC 1 television on 25 September 1987.

The composer would like to express his gratitude to Thiery Lancino, Olivier Koechlin, Robert Rowe, Corine Guironnet and Cort Lippe for their collaboration in programming and preparing the electronic part of this score.

INSTRUMENTATION

2 flutes (doubling piccolos)

2 keyboards, linked to computer [see opposite]

trombone 1 (tenor/bass)
trombone 2 (bass)

percussion (2 players):

    percussion 1

        6 anvils (imprecise pitch, but pitched
        lower than equivalent anvils of perc.2)
        (played with small metal hammers)*
        1 very large spring coil

        2 tubular bells

        4 sizzle cymbals

        3 drums (pitched higher than equivalent
        drums of perc.2) or 3 roto-toms

        * indicates pressing hammer on anvil, without re-bound

    percussion 2

        6 anvils (imprecise pitch)
        (played with small metal hammers)*
        1 large spring coil

        2 tubular bells (*not* an octave higher)

        very large bass drum

        7 maracas: 4 "suspended" in foam rubber
        3 hand-held (resting on a stand)

        3 drums or 3 roto-toms

3 violins
2 violas
2 cellos
1 double bass (with 5th string, or B extension)

    Parts are available from the publishers on hire

    Duration: *ca.* 20 minutes

For this commission the composer was invited by IRCAM to create a work utilising their 4X computer, and this was the computer used at the premiere performance. Alternatives have subsequently become available, including the NeXT computer and associated requirements, the specification for which at the time this score is published in 1993 is as follows:

Mixing Board and Artifical Reverberation
Keyboard List
    2 KX88 Yamaha keyboards
    4 volume pedals
    2 sustain pedals
    3 MIDI cables
    1 MIDI merge box
    1 MIDI interface
Computer List
    I NeXT Cube with 68040 processor
    NeXTStep 2.0 or 3.0
    8 Mbytes of memory (minimum)
    20 Mbytes of free hard disk space
ISPW List
    3 ISPW cards
    3 ProPort convertor boxer with external clock synchronisation system

All enquiries regarding this specification or other current technology appropriate for the realization of the work should be directed to the publishers or to IRCAM, 31 rue Saint-Merri, 75004 Paris, France.

PROGRAMME NOTE

During the summer of 1984 I attended the six week educational course at IRCAM. Whenever I left the Institute I found the square in front of the Pompidou Centre ringing with the sound of panpipes. A South American group would busk there every day playing their traditional music, and it was striking to see that huge, metallic building completely dominated by the sound of those little bamboo tubes.

Antara is an ancient Inca word for panpipe, a term still in use today in Peru. And the history of the panpipes is indeed ancient, with roots dating back thousands of years around the world, not only from South America, but also China, the Pacific and Southern Europe. There is an equally large variety of panpipes still in existence today, ranging from big single tubes to rows of small whistles.

Panpipes have many qualities which have been lost to today's concert instruments, amongst them a vibrant rawness and freshness of timbre. However, panpipes also have many severe constraints, including great limitations on pitch mobility and velocity. Long held notes are impossible, as are large chords. Even some melodic lines cause considerable difficulty as, on larger tubes, they have to be shared between two or more players (a technique akin to 'hocketing' in medieval music). The computer can solve all these problems and more, and so in this piece the sound of the oldest of all wind instruments has been recorded and transferred to the most modern of computers, initially the IRCAM 4X, creating an instrument ranging from the equivalent of panpipes 20 metres high to pipes of only a few millimetres. These are played via two Yamaha keyboards, which are surrounded by an ensemble of fourteen players.

At first the panpipes are used entirely melodically, almost naturally, and they encounter and communicate with two modern flutes. The flutes themselves often play in a manner akin to their ancient predecessors, hocketing melodies from left to right with almost no vibrato and a breathy sonority. (Only later in the piece does the playing style of the modern flute begin to evolve.) Eight strings act as a background to these confrontations, often in the form of a dance-like accompaniment.

This active, energetic music is threatened by two deep, growling trombones and two percussionists, the latter playing almost exclusively a plethora of anvils. These forces invoke the real power of the computerised keyboards – huge sustained microtonal chords, sweeping glissandi, breath-like sounds, percussive timbres – all derived from the original panpipes. At the largest climax the keyboards engulf the orchestral anvils in a myriad of metallic sound, after which the opposed sound sources of metal and reed fuse, and speed towards a coruscating but tranquil conclusion.

In this piece the electronic part is played live on the keyboards, with no tape, no click-track and no electronic effects. This not only allows spontaneity and rubato in performance, but also permits a deeper integration in compositional terms between the electronic and the acoustic.

G.B.

PERFORMANCE NOTES

Flutes: Several sections for the flutes imitate panpipes. A breathy non-vibrato sonority is required, with energetically-tongued attacks and abrupt cut-offs at the end of sustained tones (with absolutely no diminuendo). The flutes can be very gently amplified in order to balance with the panpipe melodies on the keyboards.

Trombones: The trombones must be somewhat amplified, especially in large halls. Also, except in the most reverberant acoustics, they should have a substantial reverb added so as both to increase their power and to facilitate fusion with the associated bass sonorities of the keyboards.

Computerised keyboards sound sources: There are three families of sampled sound employed throughout the piece:

Timbres derived from panpipes:
(i) 'Solo' - homophonic, virtuoso panpipes.
(ii) 'Nat.' - chordal panpipes, covering many octaves, capable of wide glissandi.
(iii) 'Breath' - 'aeolian' sound, derived from panpipes played without embouchure.
(iv) 'Pizz.' - panpipe timbre, with exaggerated attack and rapid decay, almost like a plucked panpipe; capable of extremely fast tremoli.

'Anvils'
Derived from re-synthesized spectra of metal girders.

'Hybrid'
A timbre which fuses solo panpipe samples with the spectra of metal girders.

The 'Solo' panpipes should be relayed from the front loud speakers; 'Breath' and 'Pizz.' should be mixed and relayed from both sets of speakers; all remaining timbres should be relayed from the (necessarily more powerful) speakers at the back.

NOTATIONAL CONVENTIONS

Microtones
d = ¼ tone flat, $\ddagger$ = ¼ sharp, $\#$ = ¾ tone sharp.
↑ = +⅛ tone, ↓ = −⅛ tone
↟ = +1/16 tone, ↡ = −1/16 tone

Time Signatures are notated in divisions of crotchet beats. That is:
2 = 2 crotchets in a bar (conventional 2/4)
2½ = 2½ crochets (conventional 5/8)
1⅔ = 1⅔ crotchets (one crotchet + two triplet quavers)
¾ = ¾ crotchet (conventional 3/16)

Appogiaturas are to be played before the beat.

Double bass harmonics sound an octave lower than written, like 'natural' notes.

Accidentals carry through the bar.

● —— = imprecise duration of decay in keyboard parts.

Keyboard notation: The keyboards (whose distribution of keys is entirely conventional) are treated as transposing instruments, each individual key having been programmed to produce a microtonal pitch. The timbres and tunings of both keyboards are changed fourteen times during the progress of the piece, all controlled by Keyboard 1. Further information is provided in the keyboard parts.

SEATING PLAN

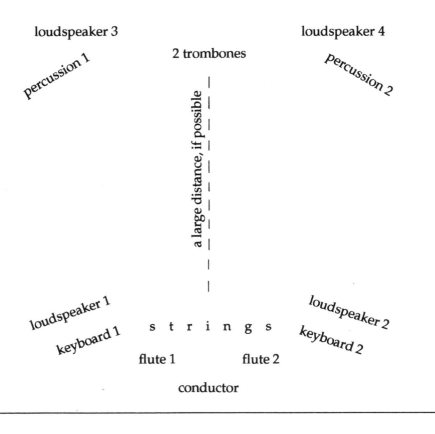

Dedicated to Tristan and Françoise Murail

ANTARA

George Benjamin

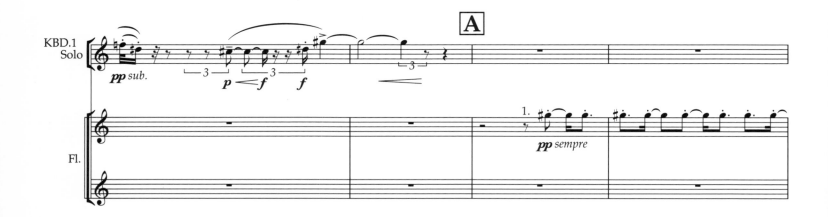

* Cello pizz: both instruments similar in sonority,
  so that their pizzicato lines fuse.

9

D **Molto ritmico, ma leggiero**

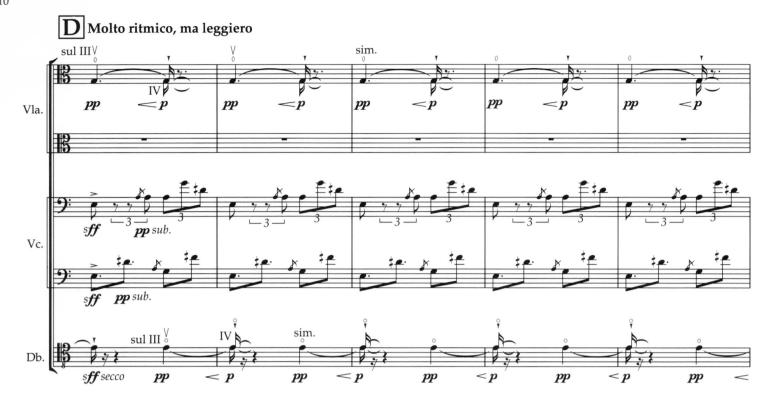

*Flutes: means wildly overblown breathy ("aeolian") timbre

14

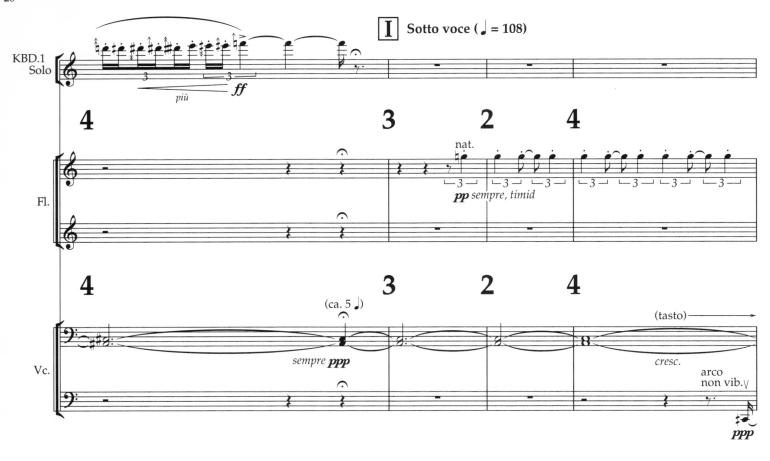

*Cello pizz: see footnote on page 7

Tempo I⁰ (♩ = 126)

* Flutes: see footnote on page 13

32

34

poco rubato

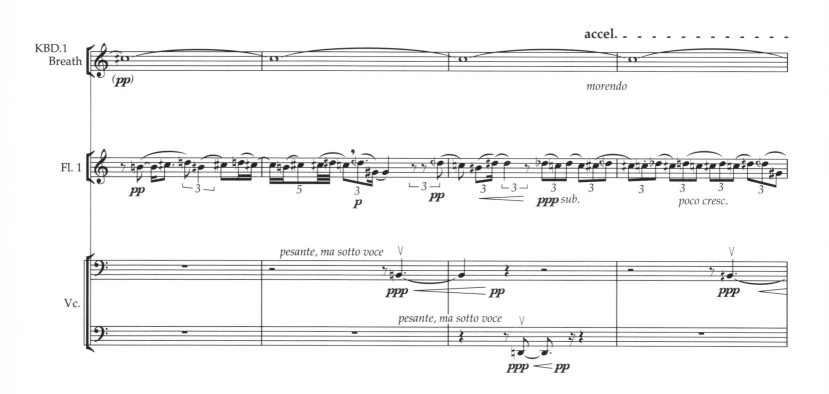

accel. poco a poco - **BB** più accel. - - - - - - - -

* From here until GG the 'Breath' timbre gradually transforms to the 'Nat.' timbre.

poco accel. - - -

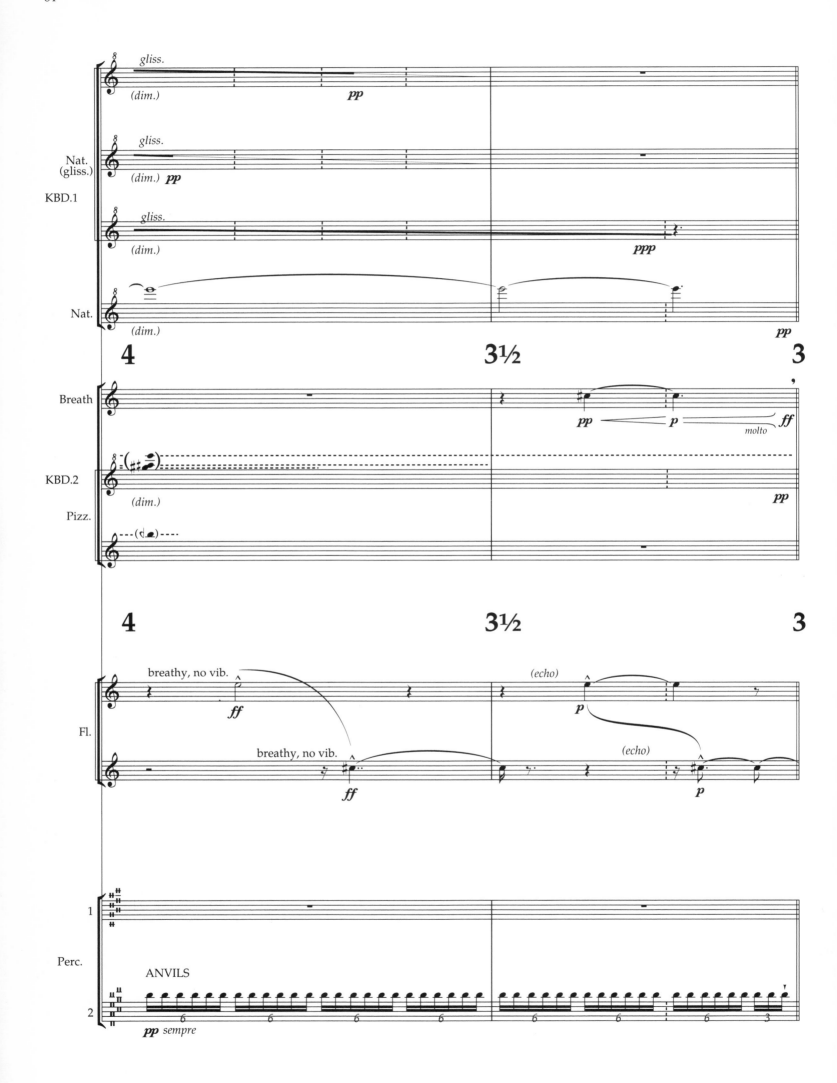

*Cellos: see footnote on page 7

*grace notes as fast as possible

NN

96

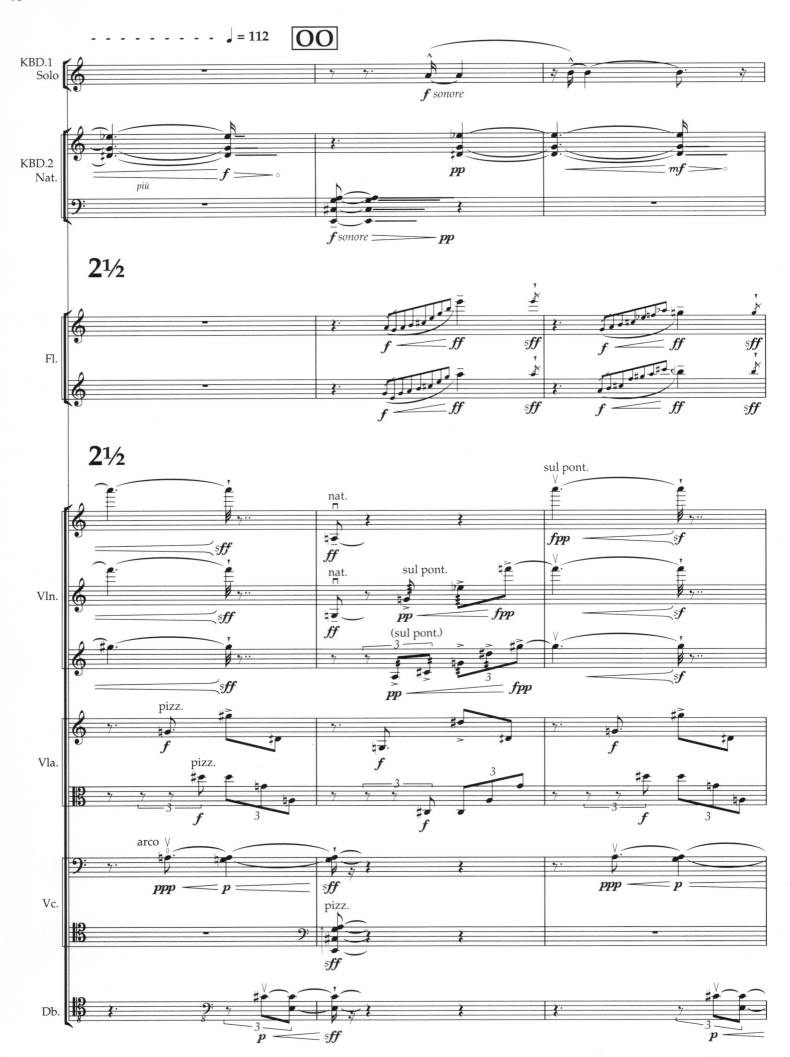

RR Rapido, ma tranquillo (♪ = 144)

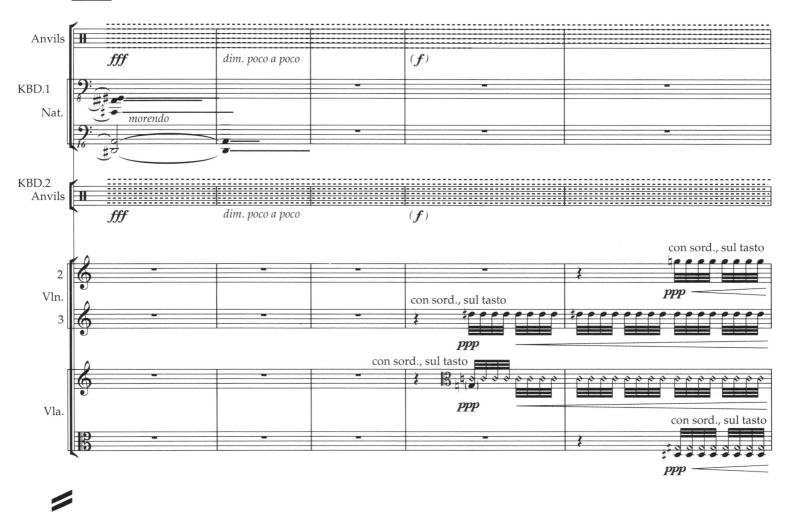

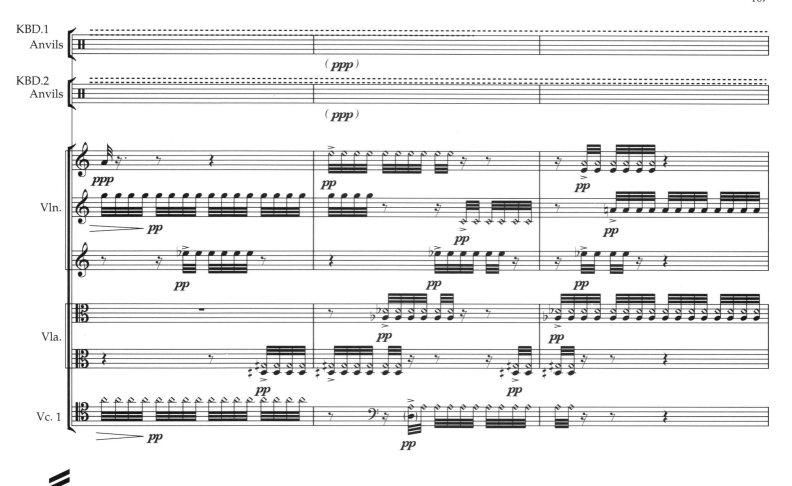

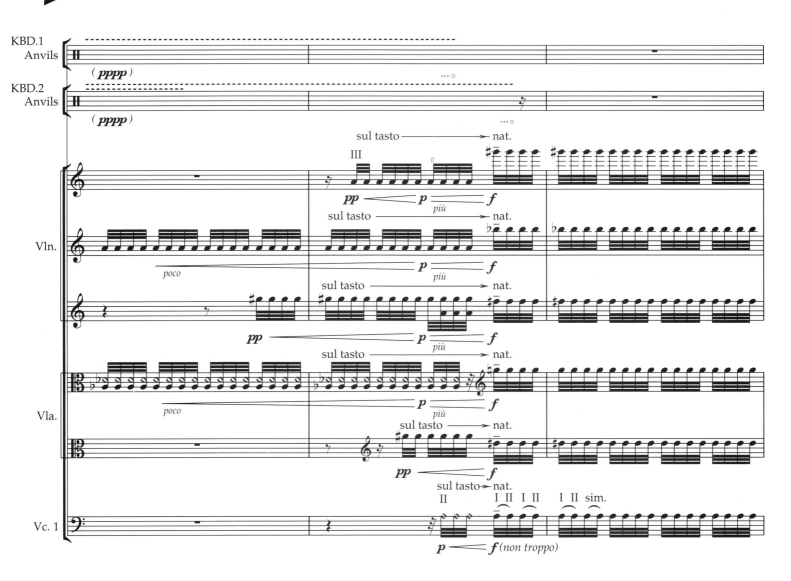

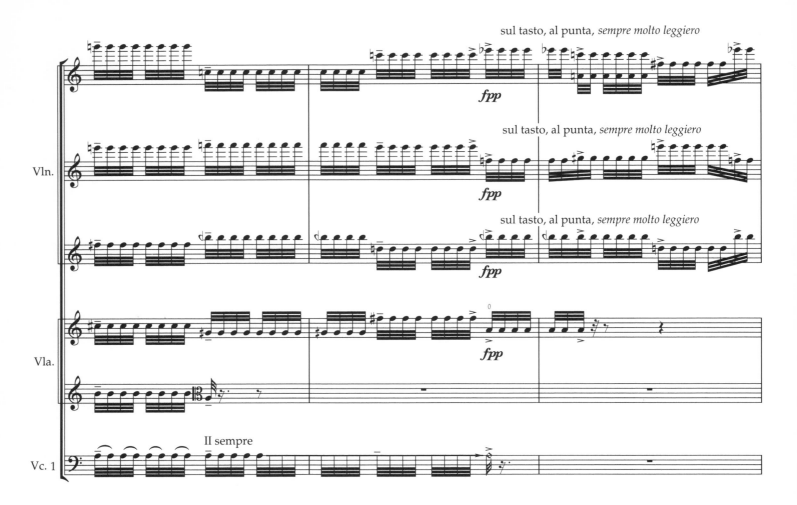

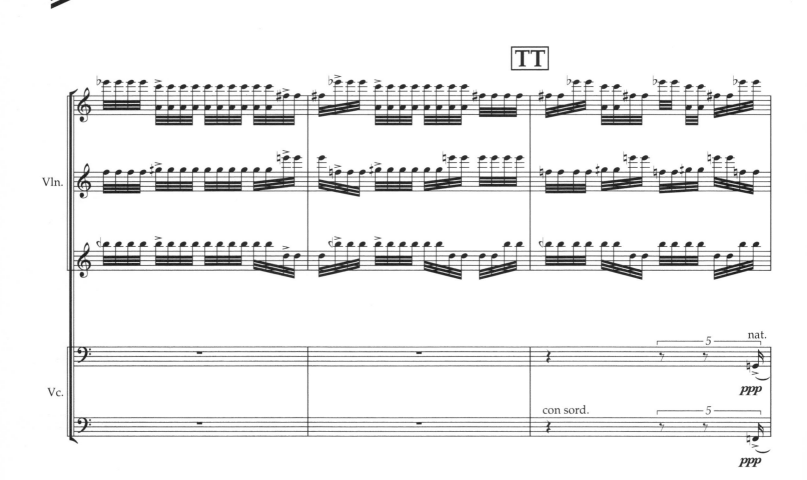

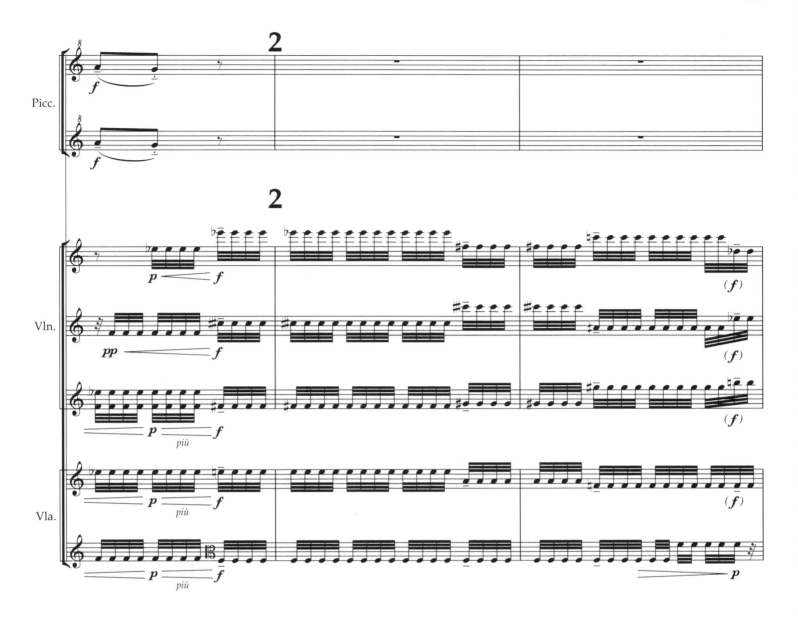

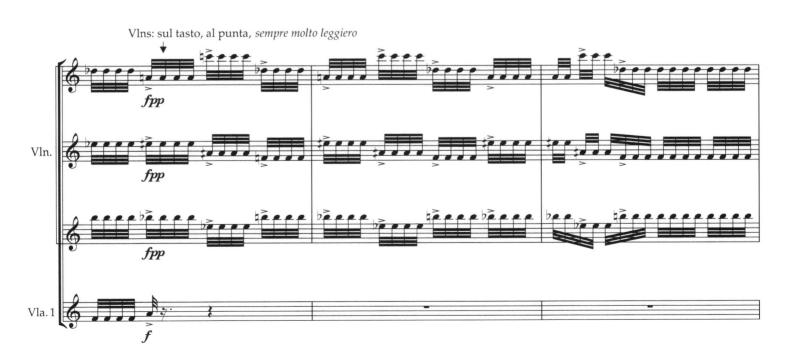

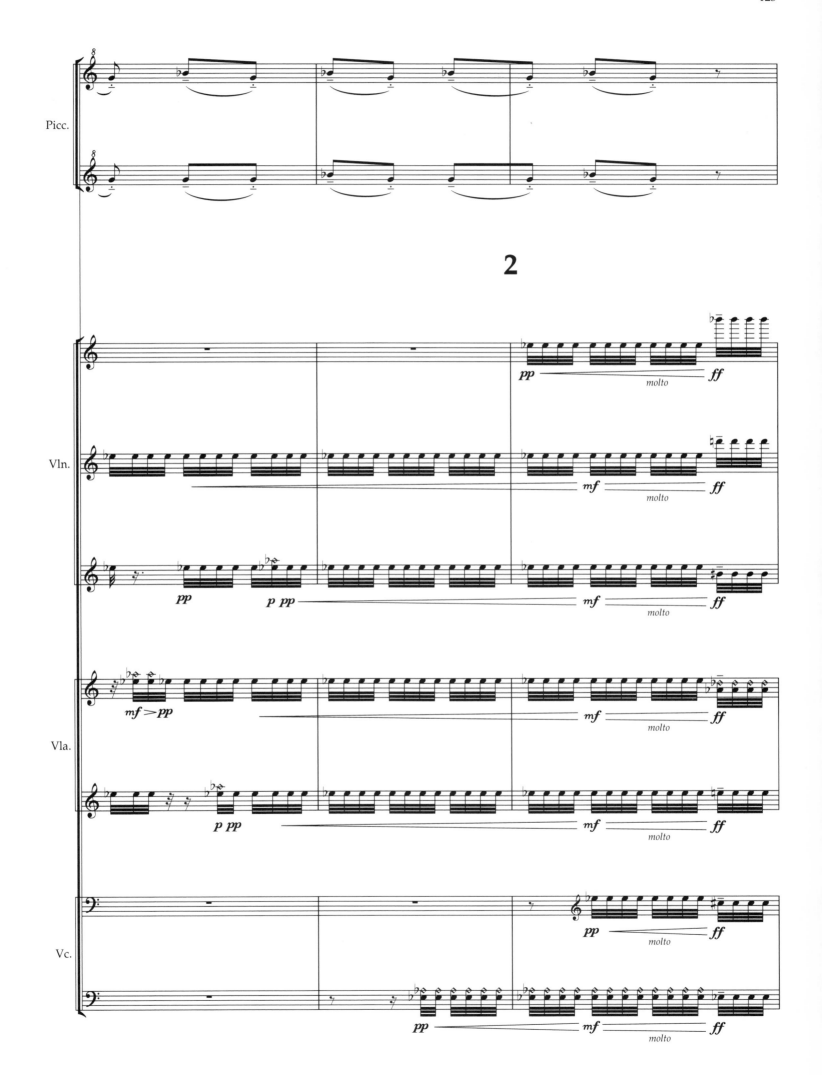

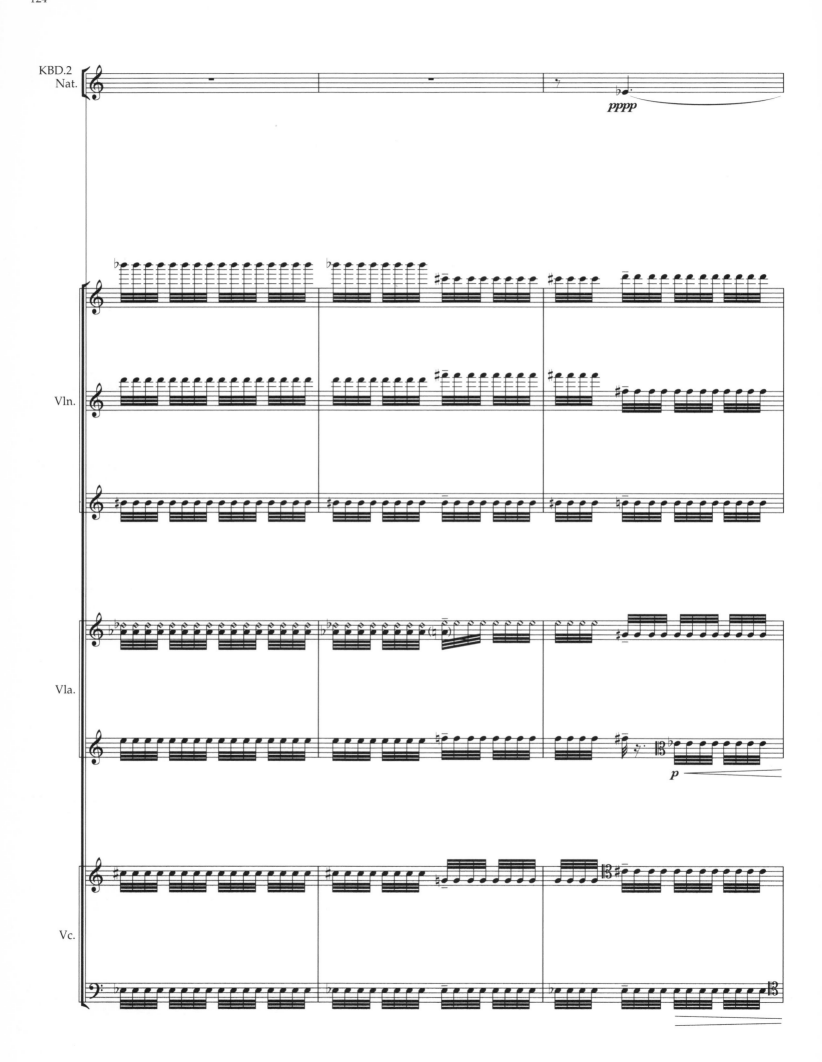

YY

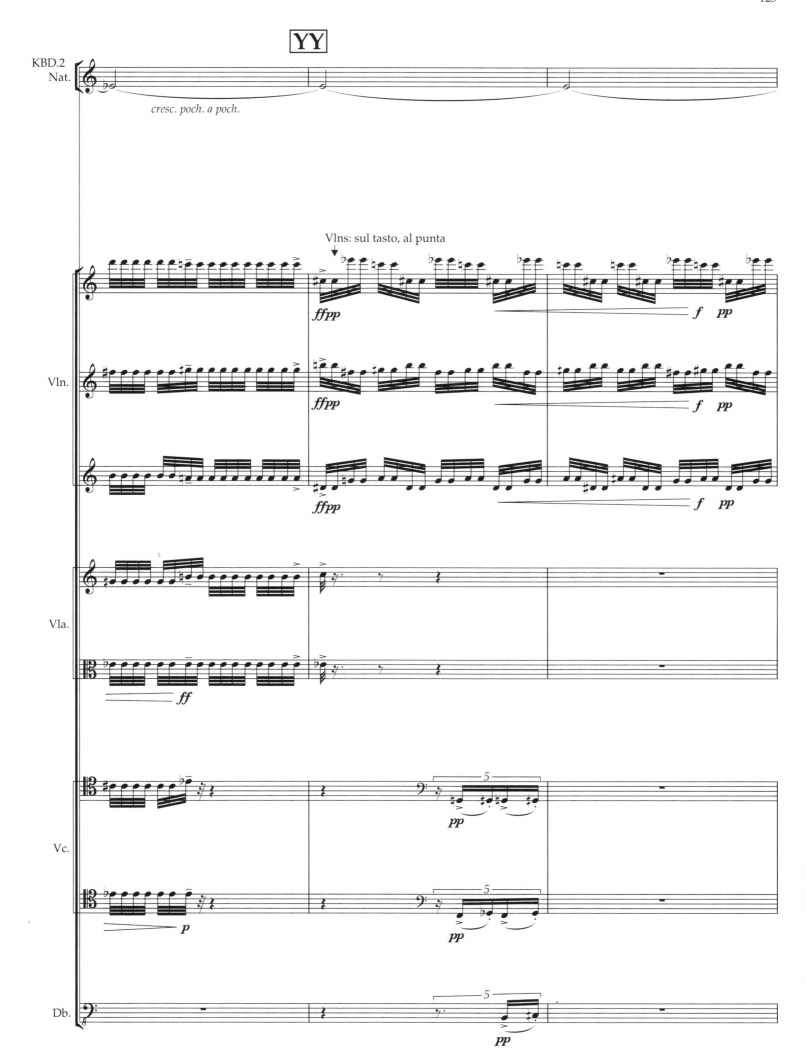

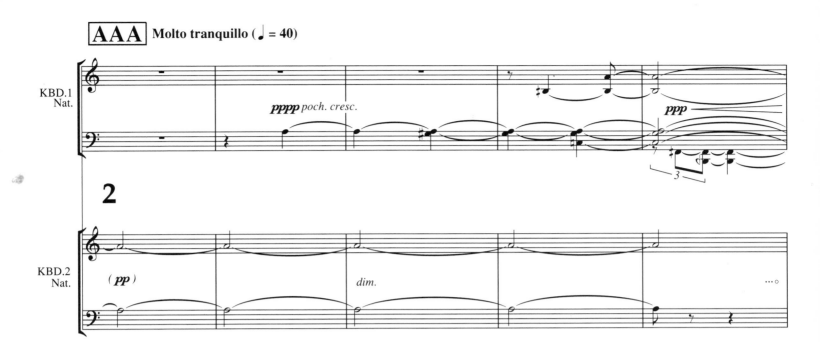

BBB

Rapido (♪ = 144)

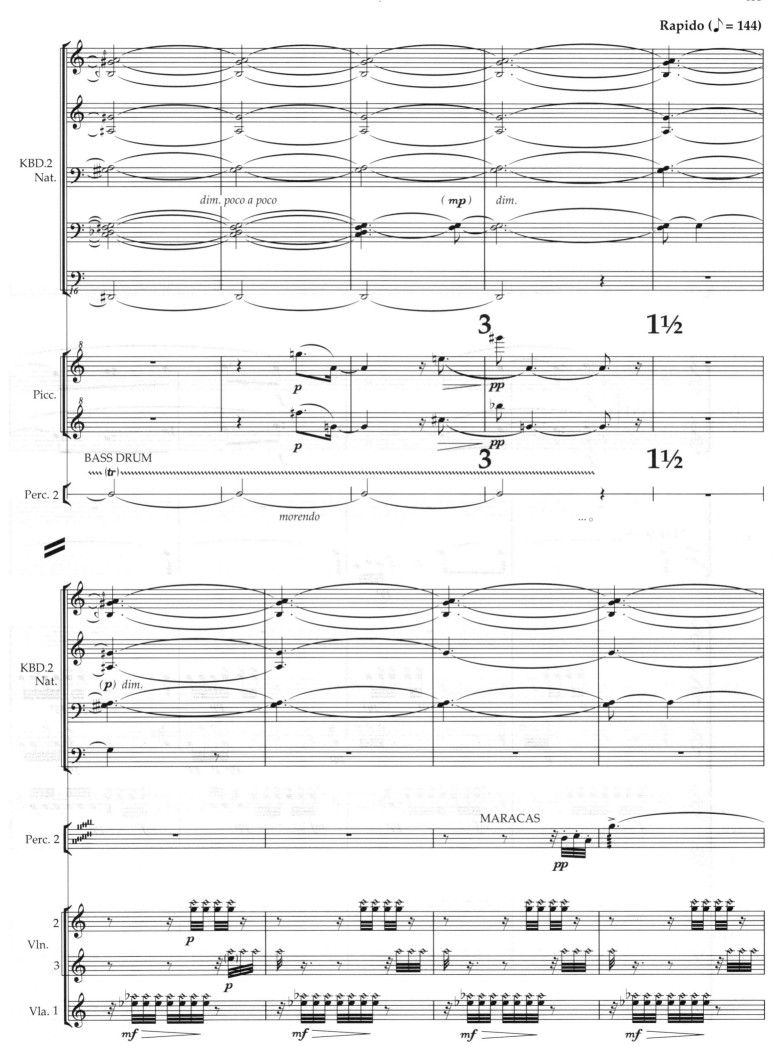

*Cymbals: l.v. notes with hands, *secco* notes with very soft beater

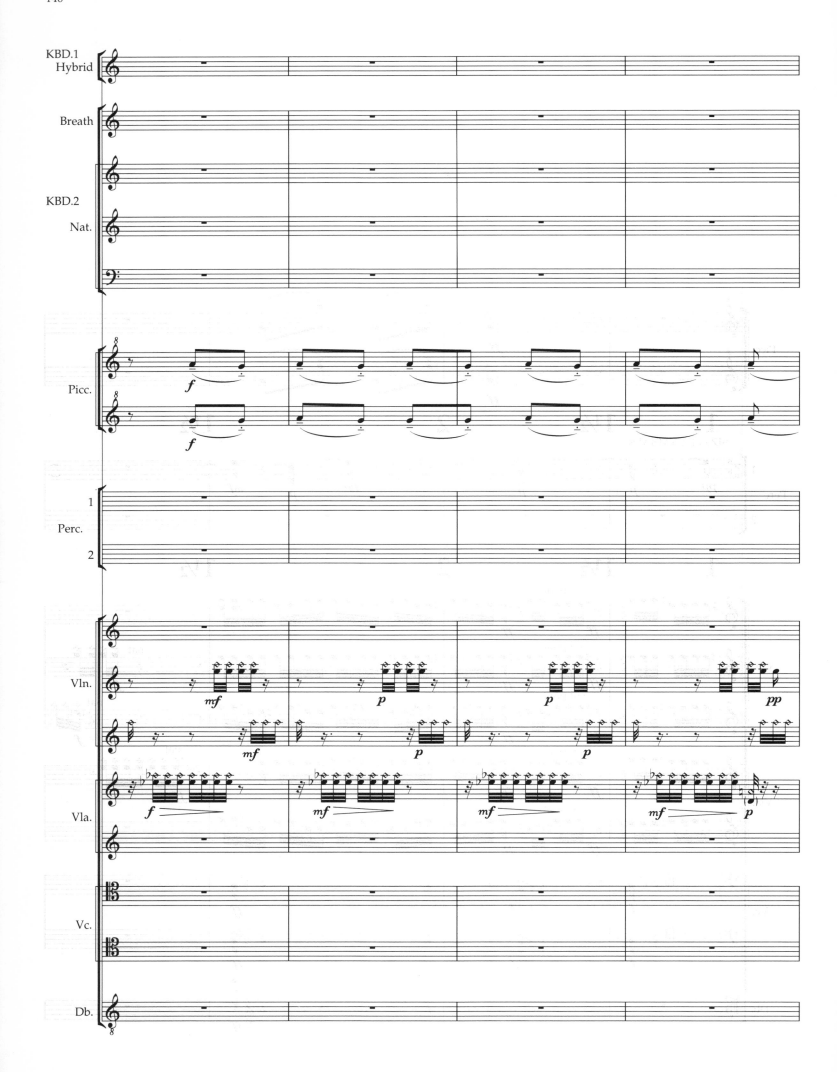

142